Unmasked

Pandemic Poems
for Children &
Exhausted Adults

by Helen Murdock-Prep

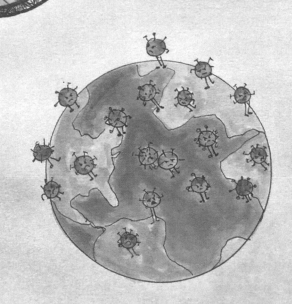

For Emma, Hanna, and Sophia Boyle
and
Elsie and Caden McCoy

With special thanks to Molly Prep,
for without her creative input and technological assistance this book would not exist.

www.instagram.com/helen.ink
www.redbubble.com/people/helenink

Also by Helen Murdock–Prep:
High Drama: A Novel
Lettering Life: Calligraphic Inspirations
Rainy Day Friend
Seasons: The Watercolors of Helen Murdock–Prep
The Time Being

ISBN: 978-0-578-29366-0

Published by Moheke Press

Moheke Press

New Friend

His mask is bright green
With frogs on the ends.
Will he like me?
Can we be friends?

I can't see his chin
Or much of his nose;
His mouth is covered
But his ears are exposed.

He waves at me,
I gasp with surprise
As I see his smile
Show up in his eyes.

During Quarantine...

I baked all the cookies
And made every cake
Ate all the pies
(Got a big belly ache.)

I learned to play drums
French horn and the flute
Trumpet, viola
And cello, to boot!

Explored every art
Through paint and Play Doh
Studied great artists
Like Klee and Van Gogh.

In a red leotard
I learned to dance
Hip Hop, Ballet
I gave each a chance.

After all this exploring
I've had my fill
I think I'll go out
And try being... still.

Starring...Us!

Little boxes
Little squares
Every day I see
My classmates stacked up
On a screen
Like we're on TV

There's my teacher!
She's the star,
She knows all her lines.
It's like we are actors
In a show
Where everybody shines.

We play our parts
As best we can.
Look, everyone should know:
I'm so proud
The year my school
Became a TV show!

Every Day

Every Day—
Zoom,
In my room:
Gloom
and
Doom!

Ode to Air

Air through my fingers,
My hair and my toes
The only place missing
Is air up my nose.

I noticed the air now
Much more than I did
I guess 'cause my mask
Seals me up like a lid.

Quarantine Pastime: My Closet

I opened up my closet
    and what do you suppose?
I decided that today
    I'd put on all my clothes.

I started with my skirts
    and every colored tee,
Dresses and coats followed
    then all pants below the knee.

It has been an hour
    I've been laying on the floor
Could you maybe, somehow
    Roll me out the door?

Thanks!

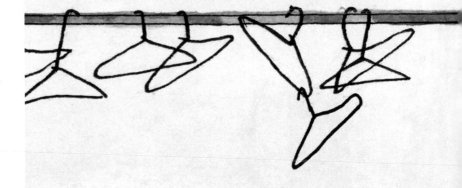

Missing

I miss my Gran
I miss my aunt
I miss my cousin Pete
I miss him lots
Even though
He has smelly feet.

I miss my pals
I miss my buds
I miss all my friends
I can't wait 'til
We're together
When this pandemic ends.

PS: I won't even complain to Pete
About his super-smelly feet!

Social Distance

I sit at my desk
Six feet from you
But jump a mile
When I hear, "ah-choo!"

Alternate Lunch

Liam B. Foster
Is up for the task
He sits at his desk
And chews on his mask.

Where Are You?

Where is COVID lurking?
That's what I want to know
Is it hiding on the sink?
Or underneath my toe?

They tell me that it's tiny
And very hard to see
That's another part
That really bothers me.

In pictures it looks big
And very, very round
With spiky things that sort of look
Like rusty nails I've found.

So, is it big? Or is it small?
I do not understand.
All I know is I'm afraid
To touch stuff with my hands.

Because if I could see it—
This bad, bad enemy
I would just avoid it.
It would be no friend to me.

Twinning

I got a new mask
I love it so much
It's purplish pink
And soft to the touch.

But what I love most,
(Aside from the hue),
When I got to Gym
My friend had one, too!

The Reveal

When you removed your mask
Your features looked out of place
You were not as I imagined
I had made up the rest of your face!

Uh Oh

Where is his mask?
It moved from his face
It's under his chin
That's not the right place!

Doesn't he know?
Didn't he hear?
There's a pandemic
It's breath that we fear

Cover that nose
Cover that mouth
Cover all air holes
From the north to the south!

From six feet away
I ask from my base
"Why isn't your mask
Covering your face?"

His eyes fly open
He looks up in shock
A wobbly smile, then,
"Sorry— I forgot!"

Behind My Mask

When I wear my mask
   I am free to be
      another kind of being
         pretending, I'm not me.

Who am I today?
   I'll give you a clue
      I used to roam the earth, but
         now I'm not in any zoo.

See my tiny arms?
   Hear my mighty roar?
      Watch me stomp around
         Yes! I'm a dinosaur!

Ode to My Mask

It's soggy
It's damp
It's stinky
It's wet
It's smelly
It's slimy
It's filled with my sweat.

What I'd like to do is squash it,
Or I can, you know, just wash it.

The New Alphabet

a-b-c-d-e-f-g,
delta-omicron-o-p,
q-r-s,
t-u-v,
w-x,
why-me?!

The New Math

One plus one
Equals two
(You'll always get this sum)

But life plus COVID
Absolutely
Adds up to, "no fun!"

The New Writing

In writing today
We were told, (and I quote),
"Write about COVID."
So here's what I wrote:

Aargh!
Aargh!
Aargh!

I looked around then
And felt a big "zing!"
'Cause all of my classmates
Wrote the same thing.

The Goo

Everything I touch
Everything I do
I keep wondering,
Is it covered with "the goo"?

That is what I'm calling
The germs I cannot see
"The goo" is hidden ickies
Shrouded in invisibility.

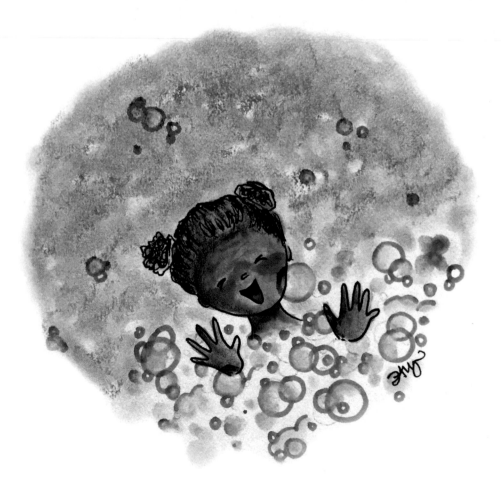

Remedy

COVID
is ugly
and spiky
and mean.
To keep
it away,
I scrub
my hands clean.

My Worry

Did you know lately
I lay in my bed
Thinking 'bout COVID
'Til I'm filled with dread?

Then I remember
With each passing day
We're one day closer
'Til it goes away.

Quarantine Craft

This stack of books
Piled so high
Will not fall down
I'll tell you why:

I glued them tight
With super glue
(You can read them
When I'm through!)

Our Quarantine Circus

Hurry, hurry, hurry
Step right up and see
The most ferocious lion
And flying dog, Jolie

Come inside the big top
Hear my parrot squawk
Stay for the main attraction
A baby who can talk!

We put on quite a show here
You couldn't ask for more
There's even popcorn and confetti
Scattered on the floor

We all love a circus
To kick away the gloom
And mom doesn't even mind
We use the living room!

The Sunny Sun

The sun beams down
The way it always did
Before the pandemic
Brought us COVID

What have you seen, sun
As you cross the sky?
Do you see us hurting?
Can you understand why?

Life went kerflooey
When this virus came
Everything changed
But you're still the same.

I am so grateful
That you rise each day
It comforts me—
Makes me feel okay.

I turn to you, sun
And give thanks from below
Standing perfectly still,
I bask in your glow.

*B.C.

I dream of a day
We go back to "before"—
Before the pandemic
Made life like a war.
Days without fighting
This invisible foe...

It all seems such a long time ago.

*Before COVID

My mind feels so mushy
Like it's filled with fog and rain.

Yes, I have that, too—
I call it "COVID brain."

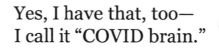
I need a hug!

XOXO

I love you
Like butter on toast
Of all we've lost
I miss hugging you most

Masking Masks Us

I miss my face
    I miss yours
It's like they're hidden
    behind doors.

I miss the smiles
    that we shared
They always showed
    how much we cared.

But my smile has changed now,
    that's the truth
While we were covered?
    I lost a tooth.

I'll show you one day
    When COVID is through
Maybe by that time
    You'll lose one, too!

The New Singing

We sing the same way,
    with each song we rejoice
By using our lungs,
    our breath and our voice.

What's different, of course,
    (I'm so glad you asked),
Is now when we're singing
    we are all masked.

We love to make music
    but it makes us pout
When we inhale those masks
    so no song can come out!

Pandemic Pastime

In the pages of this giant book
I built myself a cozy nook.
Read around me for some fun
(Just don't close it when you're done.)

I Have To Tell You Something

"We have COVID here,"
    I told my fish.
She swam close to me and asked,
    "What do you wish?"

"I wish it never happened,
    That it goes away."
She nodded in sympathy:
    "It will some day."

The New News

The new News is old news,
It's the same news each day:
COVID is mutating
And won't go away.

Escape

Let's fly away
In a great, big balloon
We'll leave COVID behind
And go live on the Moon

Don't worry 'bout us
So high in the sky
We'll eat clouds for dinner
We're leaving— goodbye!

My Question

Why is COVID such a brat?
Can someone try to answer that?!

Anyone?

Anyone?

2019

I'm on a pandemic vacation
'Cause I can't take it no more
I've gone back to ol' 2019
I time-traveled back to "before"!

So if you're tired of the changes
COVID has brought our way
Call your time-travel agent
Book your trip to the past today!

My Scholarly Dog

When school went remote
And we stayed home all day
My dog was confused
We stopped going away.

At first he just slept
On his paws at my feet
But then one day
He drew up a seat

He began taking notes
Even studied at night
He tutored me lots
Turns out, he's real bright

This went on
Day after day
'Til we took a test
And both got an "A"!

Testing Testing

I've taken tests
From grades One to Ten
All that's required
Is pencil or pen.

But this COVID test?
I'll leave to the pros
'Cause this one requires
A swab up my nose!

Looking For Answers

I climbed a mountain
    up to the sky
Found a wise man
    and asked him, "Why?"

"WHY are we suffering—
    what lies ahead?"
"This, too, shall pass,"
    is what he said.

I hurried back down
    after this interview
And told all my friends—
    now we are wise, too!

Another Pandemic Escape

I think I'll climb a rainbow,
    then use it as a slide
Colors flying past me,
    as I enjoy the ride!

Birthday Delight

My birthday celebration
    brought me lots of cheer
Even though my mom said
    no guests could come this year.

There were still balloons
    and lots of fun with you
'Cause we blew the candles out
    then split that cake in two!

Trick or Treat

I found I really caused a scene
When I dressed as COVID for Halloween!

Vaccine Blues

I tried to write a poem
About the new vaccine
But every time I started
I got to feeling mean.

That's because the subject
Had me tied in knots
'Cause the way you get this vaccine?
It's in your arm— with shots!

My Gran said it was different
When she was just a kid
They got the polio vaccine
But here is what they did:

They ate a sugar cube!
Yes, that's the greatest way.
I'd have no fear, I'd eat it up,
"More, please," I would say!

The COVID Coaster

The ups and downs of COVID
Have my brain real fried.
It's a crazy roller coaster
Please get me off this ride!

The Shortest Book

I wrote a book
About our lives now
It's just one word long...
"Wow-ee-zow-ee-ka-POW!"

Blow Me a Bubble

Blow me a bubble
Clear as can be
To keep me safe
From what's bothering me.

Hurricanes, COVID,
Power outs, bees,
Monsters (all sorts)
And falling trees.

Blow me a bubble
Where I can hide
So I can relax
All cozy inside.

If it gets lonely,
I know what to do:
I'll blow a big bubble
With room for you, too.

Even During a Pandemic...

Outside:
Snow storm
Inside:
So warm

Pondering

Out in our garden
    the flowers grow high
I lay down beneath them
    and look at the sky.

My mind starts to wander
    as the clouds roll by
I begin to wonder
    and fill up with, "Why?"

"Why did this happen?"
    I ask a bee,
"Why are we living
    this history?"

On a rock, a bird sat
    and started to sing.
That's when I realized
    this very true thing:

Though it doesn't make sense
    and we may not know why
This bee and this bird
    are with me nearby.

The Gift

Meet me at the corner
I have a gift for you
I found it in the backyard
I guess that's where it grew

Meet me at the corner
At half past two
Your gift is bursting from the box
I'm bringing hope to you!

Your turn!

Write and illustrate your own pandemic poems here:

My Imagination

I love my imagination
And use it every day
I carry it inside me
It's always ready to play

When I'm feeling lonely
I close my eyes and see
A thousand different ideas
Filled with possibility.

Be a builder of dreams

Made in United States
North Haven, CT
01 May 2022